BIGFOOT

JEN BESEL

BLACK
RABBIT
BOOKS

Bolt Jr. is published by Black Rabbit Books
P.O. Box 3263, Mankato, Minnesota, 56002.
www.blackrabbitbooks.com
Copyright © 2020 Black Rabbit Books

Grant Gould, designer; Omay Ayres, photo researcher

Names: Besel, Jennifer M., author.
Title: Bigfoot / by Jen Besel.
Description: Mankato, MN : Black Rabbit Books, 2020. |
Series: Bolt Jr. a little bit spooky |
Includes bibliographical references and index. |
Audience: Age 6-8. | Audience: K to Grade 3. Identifiers:
LCCN 2018059381 (print) | LCCN 2019005906 (ebook)
| ISBN 9781623101817 (ebook) | ISBN 9781623101756
(library binding) | ISBN 9781644661130 (paperback)
Subjects: LCSH: Sasquatch—Juvenile literature.
Classification: LCC QL89.2.S2 (ebook) |
LCC QL89.2.S2 B47 2020 (print) | DDC 001.944—dc23
LC record available at https://lccn.loc.gov/2018059381

Printed in the United States. 5/19

Image Credits

Alamy: Bill Brooks, 12–13; Buddy Mays, 6–7; Dale O'Dell, 16–17,
22–23; Friedrich Saurer, 10; United Archives GmbH, 20–21;
cnbc.com: Design Pics Inc, 5; Dreamstime: Skypixel, 18; iStock:
aleks1949, 8–9; Science Source: Spencer Sutton, 10–11; Shut-
terstock: Brody Garcia, 1; CPYstudio, 4; Rene Martin, 14 (head);
RikoBest, Cover, 13; Smartreflex, 3, 24; Tairy Greene, 21; Vitalina
Rybakova, 7 (inset)

Contents

CHAPTER 1

A Scary Sight

Rosie stands on her porch. Suddenly, she sees something. It's a huge **creature**. The creature looks at her. Then it keeps walking. She runs inside. Was that a Bigfoot?

creature: an animal, especially a nonhuman

Bigfoot ◄····
stories say
up to 12 feet
(4 meters)

**HEIGHT
COMPARISON** ····

A Big Mystery

Some people don't think Bigfoot creatures are real. Others think they are. Each year, many people say they've seen them. Sightings often happen in the woods. But no one has a good picture.

····· ▶ **grizzly bear**
up to 7 feet (2 m)

Bigfoot Features

long arms

bad smell

dirty fur

big feet

CHAPTER 2

Looking for Bigfoot

Researchers study Bigfoot stories. Most stories say the animals are covered in fur. They have long arms. They also walk on two huge feet.

researcher: someone who carefully studies something

Big Feet

People have found **footprints**. The prints are huge. Some say they're too big. No other animal could make them. Others think they're from bears.

footprint: the stamp of a foot on a surface

Where the Creatures Have Been Reported

Brazil

United States

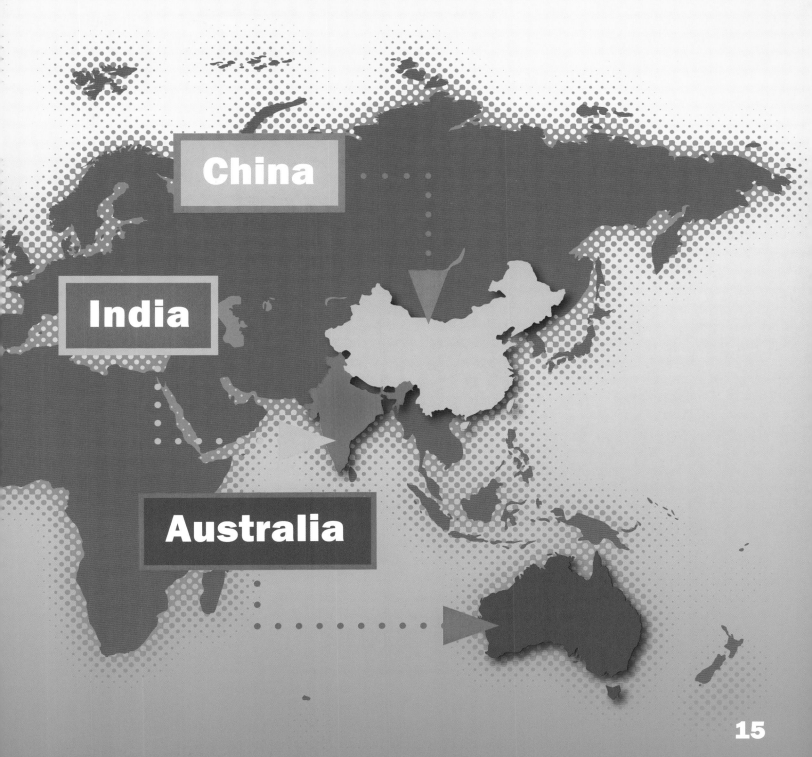

China

India

Australia

CHAPTER 3

Finding Answers

Some Bigfoot stories can be explained. Sometimes people saw bears or other animals. In 2012, scientists tested fur. Some people thought it was Bigfoot fur. But it was from common animals.

FACT

The fur came from cows, horses, and bears.

Hard to Explain

Other stories are hard to explain.
In one story, a man saw huge footprints.
Later, his sister saw a hairy creature.
It was in the same place. The creature
walked on two feet. Could that have
been a Bigfoot?

1,000

**What a Bigfoot
Might Weigh**
up to **1,000** pounds
(454 kilograms)

Bonus Facts

Some people have made fake Bigfoot footprints.

A Bigfoot's feet might be **17 inches** (43 centimeters) long.

In Australia, Bigfoot are called Yowie.

Some stories say **Bigfoot** creatures howl.

howl: to make a long, loud cry that sounds sad

21

READ MORE/WEBSITES

Gish, Ashley. *Bigfoot.* Mythical Creatures. Mankato, MN: Creative Education, 2019.

Kawa, Katie. *The Legend of Bigfoot.* Famous Legends. New York: Gareth Stevens Publishing, 2018.

Oachs, Emily Rose. *Bigfoot.* Investigating the Unexplained. Minneapolis: Bellwether Media, Inc., 2019.

North America Bigfoot Search
www.nabigfootsearch.com/home.html

Two Kids, a Camera and a Bigfoot
www.animalplanet.com/tv-shows/
finding-bigfoot/videos/two-kids-a-
camera-and-a-bigfoot

GLOSSARY

creature—an animal, especially a nonhuman

footprint—the stamp of a foot on a surface

howl—to make a long, loud cry that sounds sad

researcher—someone who carefully studies something

INDEX